T0368433

METUSELA ALBERT

SALVATION IS CONDITIONAL.

To order additional copies of this book, contact:
Xlibris
844-714-8691
www.Xlibris.com
Orders@Xlibris.com

ISBN: Softcover   979-8-3694-2855-9
         EBook   979-8-3694-2856-6

Print information available on the last page

Rev. date: 08/19/2024

Contents

NOTE: THOSE CONDITIONS MENTIONED IN THOSE 10 CHAPTERS, PROVES THE POINT THAT SALVATION IS <u>NOT</u> UNCONDITIONAL.

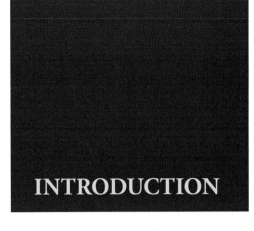

INTRODUCTION

Every religion teaches its members of a better life after death. But no religion has the truth about life after death, except Christianity which is taken from the Bible.

Eternal life through JESUS, is the hope of every Professed Christian. However, because of the many misconceptions on the subject of Salvation by many Churches, hence this Book is written to help Professed Christians fall <u>not</u> into the subtle deceptions of Satan. We will explore this subject and learn of the truth, and the truth will expose the subtle deceptions.

Many Professed Christians believe that when JESUS died at Calvary, all past, present, and future sins, were all forgiven. In other words, everyone we forgiven and given the free gift of eternal life by JESUS at Calvary. According to them, all were already forgiven and saved by that one act of JESUS at Calvary.

What does it mean? It means, the sinner does <u>not</u> have to confess or repent of sins because salvation is a free gift from JESUS at Calvary. They teach that Confession and Repentance are <u>the fruit of Salvation</u>. They advocate that the sinner confesses and repents because of the gift of Forgiveness and Salvation, <u>already received</u>. They teach that the reason the sinner obeys is because he or she was already saved. They also teach that Obedience is the fruit of Salvation. Did you get that? Wrong!

WHAT IS THE TRUTH? Obedience is the fruit of Faith, not the fruit of Salvation.

We must clarify the truth well, and condemn the false teachings.

The theology called - "Unconditional Salvation at Calvary" is advocating "Salvation <u>IN</u> Sin" rather than "Salvation <u>FROM</u> Sin."

....

THE TRUTH IS:

JESUS died at Calvary "To Save" us.

Not, JESUS died at Calvary and Saved us.

Stop right here, and make sure you know the truth stated above in order to know the error.

THE TRUTH	THE ERROR
• JESUS died at Calvary <u>to save</u> <u>us.</u>	• JESUS died at Calvary <u>and</u> <u>saved us.</u>

NOTE: The death of JESUS at Calvary did <u>not</u> give the gift of eternal life to a sinner. It is only a provision made for the sinner to be saved. The sinner has to believe in JESUS, confess and repent of sins. Repentance must precede forgiveness of sin, and the receiving of the gift of Salvation.

Compiled by: Metusela F. Albert

A <u>Provision</u> for Everyone "<u>to be saved</u>" was made at Calvary by the death of JESUS.

....

CHAPTER 1

THE UNCONDITIONAL LOVE OF GOD.

At Calvary, JESUS died _to save_ us _from_ sin and to give us the gift of eternal life. This is the <u>unconditional love</u> of GOD.

JESUS IS GOD. It was JESUS who first loved us and condescended to become a human being like us and to die at Calvary to give eternal life to mankind.

JESUS did _not_ have to die. HE could have ordered an angel to die instead of HIM. But an angel cannot atone for our sins since the holy law of GOD was transgressed. Only JESUS, the JEHOVAH, who wrote the law can make the atonement for sin.

....

After Adam and Eve sinned, JESUS had to use a lamb to die in their behalf as the sacrifice. Otherwise, they would have been dead immediately after their eating of the fruit of the tree of the knowledge of good and evil. The lamb died instead of Adam and Eve. The lamb was symbolic of JESUS who later came and died at Calvary as our Sin Bearer / Savior. When JESUS died, that was the end of animal sacrificial offerings. The death of JESUS did not change the Ten Commandments. Not one commandment was abolished or changed at Calvary by JESUS' death.

If Adam and Eve had died immediately after the eating of the forbidden fruit, they can't confess and repent of their sins. And eventually, they would die the eternal death which is the wages of sin because they were not alive to confess and repent – Romans 6:23.

To give an example. If you were living in sin, and had a sudden death by accident, you would die the eternal death which is the wages of sin – Romans 6:23.

While we are alive, we have the opportunity to confess and repent of our sins. Today is the day of Salvation. Tomorrow may not come. Stop procrastinating.

....

The lamb killed at Eden after Adam and Eve's fall was <u>symbolic</u> of JESUS who later became the sacrifice at Calvary. HE died to save us.

....

JESUS who was GOD cannot die. Therefore, He humbly took the INCARNATION process through Mary at Bethlehem and became <u>human like us to enable Him to die at Calvary</u>. So, when JESUS died at Calvary, it was His <u>human nature</u> that died, <u>not His divine nature</u>. His humanity died at Calvary, <u>not</u> his divinity.

....

NOTE: While we were living in sin, GOD still loved us. That does <u>not</u> mean, HE gave us the gift of eternal life unconditionally.

ILLUSTRATION.

While King David was committing adultery with Bathsheba (the wife of Uriah), both were <u>not</u> saved.

And when King David killed Uriah, he was <u>not</u> saved.

Not till King David <u>confessed and repented</u> of his sins committed, then he was forgiven and saved.

You can read of King David's confession and repentance in Psalms 32 and 51.

....

1 John 1:9 says – "If we <u>confess</u> our sins, JESUS is faithful and just to <u>forgive</u> us and to cleanse us from all unrighteousness."

NOTE: <u>Confession</u> and <u>Repentance</u> must *precede* the receiving of the gifts of <u>Forgiveness</u> and <u>Salvation</u>, from GOD.

The gift of forgiveness will always precede the gift of Salvation. Once the gift of forgiveness is granted by GOD, then the gift of eternal life (Salvation) will follow automatically.

....

SALVATION IS CONDITIONAL.

FACT: No sinner will be given the gift of forgiveness and eternal life without confession and repentance.

There is nothing impossible for GOD, but He will <u>not</u> forgive a sinner who does <u>not</u> confess and repent of sins.

Read Ezekiel 18:18-20.

»»»

HERE IS THE THING.

If GOD forgives a sinner who does not confess and repent, then He would have to forgive Satan and one-third of the angels who were cast out of heaven due to disobedience. Then GOD would have to re-instate them back to heaven.

Have you ever thought seriously about that?

Think folks, the "Unconditional Salvation" doctrine is Satanic. Stop rewarding Satan and the evil angels.

Try and condemn the false doctrine if your Church is teaching that Satanic doctrine. Perhaps, your friends in the Church did not know the false doctrine. Since you knew it now, then condemn it. Try and share with your friends. Don't be afraid to stand up for JESUS and tell the truth. At the same time, tell the errors and the false teachings. Create programs to educate everyone in different Churches. Make use of your social media account to share the truth.

I committed my time to write Books. When I am dead, the Books will remain in the Book Stores as a witness for the Truth. Whether the people believe it or not, that is not the issue.

CHAPTER 2

BELIEVING IS A CONDITION

Scripture Reading: John 3:16, 18. (KJV).

v16. "For God so loved the world, that he gave his only begotten Son, that whosoever <u>believeth</u> in him should not perish, but have everlasting life."

v18. He that <u>believeth in him is not condemned</u>: but he that <u>believeth not is condemned already</u>, because he hath <u>not believed</u> in the name of the only begotten Son of God.

....

Another Scripture Reading: Romans 4:4 & 5. KJV.

V4. Now to him that worketh is the reward not reckoned of grace, but of debt.

V5. But to him that worketh not, but <u>believeth</u> on him that justifieth the ungodly, <u>his faith</u> is counted for righteousness.

....

....

NOTE: There is <u>no</u> Salvation to anyone who does not <u>believe</u> in JESUS who came and died at Calvary as the world's Sin Bearer / Savior.

....

NOTE: THIS IS VERY IMPORTANT TO UNDERSTAND THE DIFFERENCE BETWEEN <u>BELIEVE</u> FROM <u>FAITH</u> AND <u>SAVING FAITH</u>.

....

To "<u>BELIEVE</u>" is to have <u>a mental assent</u> to a certain information. For example, to <u>believe</u> in JESUS as our Savior, is to do with your <u>mental</u> acceptance.

To have "FAITH" in JESUS, is to do with <u>TRUST</u> in Him.

But "SAVING FAITH" is more than TRUSTING JESUS. It is the kind of TRUST that is willing to <u>OBEY</u> JESUS despite all odds.

When Abraham expressed his faith to take Isaac and sacrifice on Mount Moriah, that is a SAVING FAITH. His faith expressed Obedience. When Faith goes hand in hand with Obedience, that is Saving Faith.

Though Abraham did not know where he was going, yet he obeyed God's leading. Saving Faith is to obey God whatever the cost. (Genesis 12:1-5).

If Abraham were to sacrifice his son Isaac, then how is the promise that his descendants would be like the sand of the sea? He was willing to obey God and reasoned that since God gave him Isaac at his Old age, therefore, God is able to resurrect him after the sacrifice. THAT IS SAVING FAITH. (Genesis 22:1-18, Hebrews 11:18-19).

....

CHAPTER 3

FAITH IS A CONDITION

If you don't believe in JESUS who died at Calvary to be our Sin Bearer, then surely you won't have faith in Him who can forgive your sins. Thus, Salvation is <u>not</u> going to be granted.

Faith is an important element to proceed in line toward the gift of Forgiveness and Salvation from GOD.

Let's read the Scriptures about the <u>Faith</u> of the Patriarchs.

Hebrews 11:6. But without <u>faith</u>; it is impossible to please him; for he that cometh to God must <u>believe</u> that he is, and that he is a rewarder of them that diligently seek him.

Hebrews 11:7. By <u>faith</u> Noah, being warned of God of things not seen as yet, moved with fear, prepared an ark to the saving of his house; by the which he condemned the world, <u>and became heir of the righteousness which is by faith.</u>

Hebrews 11:8. By <u>faith</u> Abraham, when he was called to go out into a place which he should after receive for an inheritance, <u>obeyed</u>, and he went out, not knowing whither he went.

Hebrews 11:9. By <u>faith</u> he sojourned in the land of promise, as in a strange country, dwelling in tabernacles with Isaac and Jacob, the heirs with him of the same promise:

Hebrews 11:10. For he looked for a city which hath foundations, whose builder and maker is God.

....

Hebrews 11:11. Through <u>faith</u> also Sara herself, received strength to conceive seed, and was delivered of a child when she was past age, because she judged him faithful who had promised.

....

Hebrews 11:27. By faith he (Moses) forsook Egypt, not fearing the wrath of the king: for he endured, as seeing who is invisible.

Hebrews 11:28. Through faith he (Moses) kept the Passover, and the sprinkling of blood, lest he that destroyed the firstborn should touch them.

Hebrews 11:29. By faith they passed through the Red Sea as by dry land: which the Egyptians assaying to do were drowned.

Hebrews 11:30 By faith the walls of Jericho fell down, after they were compassed about seven days.

Hebrews 11:31 By faith the harlot Rahab perished not with them that believed not, when she had received the spies with peace.

....

CHAPTER 4

CONFESSION IS A CONDITION.

Scripture Reading - 1 John 1:9

"If we <u>confess</u> our sins, JESUS is faithful and just to forgive us our sins and to cleanse us from all unrighteousness."

....

Confession from the sinner must precede the receiving of the gift of forgiveness from GOD. Without confession, there is <u>no</u> forgiveness. And without forgiveness, there is <u>no</u> salvation.

....

The sinner, the one who transgressed God's law, must confess his or her sins to GOD before GOD grants the gift of forgiveness. You can confess your sins to GOD at any time of the day or night, and from wherever you are.

Disobedient JONAH confessed and repented while he was in the belly of the fish out in the deep sea. And God answered his prayer. God then directed the fish to take him to the beach at Nineveh, and spewed him on the shore.

CAUTION: YOU DO NOT HAVE TO WAIT FOR SUNDAY TO GO TO A CONFESSION BOX AT A CHURCH BUILDING TO CONFESS YOUR SINS, TO A PRIEST.

....

NOTE: You are not required to pay money for your confession of sins. There is no such thing as a Confession Box or Window.

Go to JESUS and Confess your sins to him, at any time of the day from anywhere.

If you wronged someone, make reconciliation with him or her. But if you transgressed God's law, confess your sins to JESUS who can forgive you and give you the gift of eternal life.

CHAPTER 5

REPENTANCE IS A CONDITION.

Scripture Reading –

Luke 15:7 & 10 (KJV).

v7. Jesus said, "I say unto you, that likewise joy shall be in heaven over one sinner that <u>repenteth</u>, more than over ninety and nine just persons, which need no repentance."

v10. Jesus said again, "Likewise, I say unto you, there is joy in the presence of the angels of God over one sinner that <u>repenteth</u>."

In the parable of the lost sheep, lost coin, lost son, JESUS makes the point about Salvation. There is no Salvation to the sinner without repentance. He repeated it twice.

1. The lost coin does not know that it is lost. Therefore, it was the owner that searched for it and brought it back. # 2. The lost sheep knows that it is lost but does not know how to go back to the sheep-pen (fold).

3. The lost son knew that he was lost while at the pig farm and made the decision to return home from where he was. He genuinely confessed his sins and repented in his heart, and the Father knew. God saw his mind / heart and ran to meet him and made a party for him. The calf was killed.

In Luke 15, the parable started with the accusation by the Pharisees and the Scribes that JESUS was mingling and eating with sinners.

Twice, JESUS emphasized that there will be joy in heaven over one sinner that <u>repents (verses 7 & 10)</u>.

JESUS condemned the ninety-nine just persons who feel no need of repentance. HE alluded this group to the Pharisees and the Scribes who feel they are the righteous and no need to repent.

Therefore, Salvation is <u>not</u> going to be granted to a sinner who does <u>not</u> repent.

Since Salvation is <u>not</u> without Repentance, therefore, there is no such thing as Unconditional Salvation at Calvary.

....

....

CHAPTER 6

LOVE AND OBEDIENCE ARE CONDITIONS.

In John 14:15, JESUS said, "If ye love me, <u>keep</u> my commandments."

When you love JESUS and keep His commandments, you are <u>not</u> a legalist.

But if you obey GOD to earn Salvation, that is legalistic.

The Pharisees were legalists. They believed that Salvation can be earned by the keeping of the Ten Commandments. Therefore, they tried to keep the Ten Commandments without believing in JESUS who was the lawgiver.

JESUS wants us to keep His commandments because we <u>love</u> Him. Love for GOD should be the motivating factor for our desire to keep the Ten Commandments.

We cannot keep the Ten Commandments without the help of JESUS. With JESUS, we can faithfully keep the Ten Commandments.

REMEMBER, in Matthew 5:48, JESUS said, "Be ye therefore perfect, even as your Father which is in heaven is perfect."

Romans 2:13 – "For not the hearers of the law are just before God, but the <u>doers</u> of the law shall be justified".

....

Genesis 22:18.

God said to Abraham - "And in thy seed shall all the nations of the earth be blessed; because thou hast <u>obeyed</u> my voice."

....

NOTE: It was the descendants of Abraham through Isaac that came Mary who gave birth to the humanity of JESUS at Bethlehem through the INCARNATION process. JESUS was from the lineage of Isaac, <u>not</u> of Ishmael.

OBEDIENCE TO GOD IS VITAL.

If your faith is not strong enough to produce OBEDIENCE, then your faith is dead.

NO SINNER WILL BE SAVED WHILE LIVING IN DISOBEDIENCE TO GOD.

- In John 14:15, JESUS said,"If ye <u>love me</u>, <u>keep my commandments</u>" KJV.

- In Revelation 22:14, JESUS said "Blessed are they that <u>do</u> his commandments, that they may have right to the tree of life, and may enter in through the gates into the city."KJV.

Compiled by: Metusela F. Albert.

....

....

CHAPTER 7

OBEDIENCE IS THE FRUIT OF FAITH, NOT THE FRUIT OF SALVATION.

When you hear a Pastor teaches; "Obedience is the Fruit of Salvation", know for sure that it is a heresy. It is very simple to see the error once you knew the truth.

WHY THE BELIEF THAT SAYS, "OBEDIENCE IS THE FRUIT OF SALVATION," IS HERETICAL?

This belief promotes the idea that a sinner is saved, before he or she obeys God's commandments.

It teaches that the sinner is willing to obey God because he or she was already saved at Calvary. He or she obeys God's commandments <u>not to be saved</u>, but because Salvation has already been granted at Calvary unconditionally.

....

ACCORDING TO THE BELIEF THAT SAYS, "YOU WERE ALREADY SAVED AT CALVARY UNCONDITIONALLY," THUS, OBEDIENCE IS ONLY A RESPONSE TO YOUR SALVATION, NOT TO BE SAVED.

LET'S ANALISE IT.

1. If you were already saved at Calvary without obedience, then you do not need to obey God. This is Satanic.

2. If everyone were already saved at Calvary, then it does not matter how you live your life, yet you will be taken to heaven without obedience to God. That is Satanic.

3. According to that theory, you can kill as many people, yet you will end up in heaven. That is Satanic.

4. According to that theory, everyone will go to heaven, and none will go to hell. That is Satanic.

5. According to that theory, you can steal all your life, and expect to go to heaven.

6. According to that theory, you can worship idols, yet expect to go to heaven. That is Satanic.

7. According to that theory, you can have many wives at the same time, yet expect to go to heaven with all your wives. That is Satanic.

8. According to that theory, idol worship, adultery, fornication, stealing, killing, etc., are <u>not</u> issues of sin. That is Satanic.

....

THE TRUTH: OBEDIENCE IS THE FRUIT OF FAITH.

Your faith will lead you <u>to obey</u> God's commandments <u>before</u> the gift of Salvation is granted by him.

....

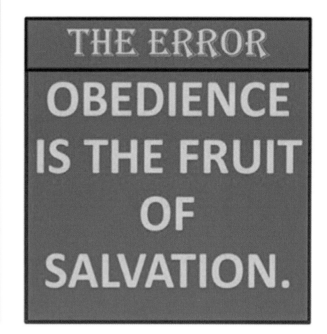

Compiled by: Metusela F. Albert.

NOTE: Love for God's love is the motivating power for the sinner to obey His Commandments. This is not a Pharisaic legalistic obedience.

Another reason the OBEDIENCE of the Pharisees is legalistic is – they try to keep the Commandments but did not believe in JESUS who came in human flesh through Mary at Bethlehem as the Messiah, prophesied in the Book of Isaiah 7:14; and 9:6. They did not believe.

Any obedience to God's Commandments without believing in Christ, as the Messiah, is a Pharisaical law keeping type.

We are told by JESUS to keep the Commandments.

....

YOU CAN'T BE SAVED UNLESS YOU KEEP THE COMMANDMENTS OF GOD. JESUS SAID.

- Matthew 19:16 -17. KJV.

- v16 – **And, behold, one came and said unto him, Good Master, what good thing shall I do, that I may have eternal life?**

- v17 – **And he said unto him, Why callest thou me good: there is none good but one, that is, God: <u>but if thou wilt enter unto life, keep the commandments</u>. . . .**

Further reading: - John 14:15; Revelation 22:11-14.

Compiled by: Metusela F. Albert

. . . .

IF you did not understand the point stated above, then read these two Scriptures to further prove the above point.

NO SINNER WILL BE SAVED WHILE LIVING IN DISOBEDIENCE TO GOD.

- In John 14:15, JESUS said, "If ye <u>love me</u>, <u>keep my commandments</u>" KJV.

- In Revelation 22:14, JESUS said "Blessed are they that <u>do</u> his commandments, that they may have right to the tree of life, and may enter in through the gates into the city. KJV.

Compiled by: Metusela F. Albert.

TAKE NOTE OF THE TRUTH:

THE SINNER'S OBEDIENCE TO GOD MUST <u>PRECEDE</u> THE RECEIVING OF THE GIFTS OF <u>FORGIVENESS AND SALVATION.</u>

REMEMBER, GOD SEES THE HEART. YOUR WILLINGNESS TO OBEY GOD MUST START IN <u>YOUR MIND, IN WHICH THE BIBLE REFERS TO THE HEART.</u> (This point must be understood well).

A VERY CRUCIAL POINT.

Read John 14:15 and Revelation 22:14, and understand it well.

Since JESUS said those words, try and memorize them, and you will protect yourself from <u>the false teaching</u> that says, "Salvation is Unconditional."

Another false teaching about Salvation, says, "Salvation is by Faith alone," meaning without the Obedience to God's law."

//

CHAPTER 8

FAITH WITHOUT WORKS IS DEAD.

Scripture Reading: James 2:17, 20-21.

V17. Even so faith, if it hath not works, is dead, being alone.

V20. But wilt thou know, O vain man, that faith without works is dead?

V21. Was not Abraham our father justified by works, when he had offered Isaac his own son upon the altar?

....

Your faith must bear the fruit of your works. Faith without works is dead. Faith alone is dead.

Faith without Obedience is dead.

Abel's faith was seen by his works (obedience), when he brought a lamb to sacrifice.

Noah's faith was seen by his obedience to God, to build the Ark before the flood happened.

Abraham's faith was seen by his obedience to God, when asked to leave his relatives and to go to another country that he did not know. (Genesis 12:1-5).

Abraham's faith was seen by his works of <u>obedience</u> to sacrifice his son, Isaac, on Mount Moriah – (Genesis 22).

....

<u>FAITH AND WORKS</u> GO HAND IN HAND.

Both complement each other. You will know them by their fruits. Their works will testify of their faith.

Their belief in God will stretch beyond the mental assent to the point of willingness to obey what God commanded them to do. Nothing can stop them from obeying God. Yes, God comes first. Obedience to God is the fruit of Faith. (NOTE: Salvation is NOT the fruit of Faith).

Try and read the faith of the Patriarchs in the Book of Hebrews Chapter 11 in the New Testament.

///

CHAPTER 9

WHAT MUST I DO TO HAVE ETERNAL LIFE?

Wow! What a question.

That question needs to be answered well. And we will let JESUS answer it for us, then we can rest the case in good hands. Amen?

....

Dear Christian Brothers and Sisters, stay tuned and fasten your seat belts.

Our "SALVATION FLIGHT" met lots of rough turbulences for quite a long time. Nevertheless, we are preparing for landing by God's grace. Thank you for choosing to fly with us, and looking forward to seeing you again in the near future. Don't hesitate to check my other Ten Books online at www.amazon.com OR www.xlibris.com.

So, let's read the answer by JESUS to the Jewish Rich Young Ruler's question.

Read Matthew 19:16 & 17.

v16. And, behold, one came and said unto him,

Good Master, what good thing shall I do, that I may have eternal life?

v17. And he said unto him, Why callest me good? There is none good but one, that is, God: but if thou wilt enter into life, keep the commandments.

....

DID YOU NOTICE WHAT JESUS SAID?

Keeping the commandments is a requirement to be saved. JESUS said it.

YOU CAN'T BE SAVED UNLESS YOU KEEP THE COMMANDMENTS OF GOD. JESUS SAID.

- Matthew 19:16-17
- v16 – And, behold, one came and said unto him, Good Master, what good thing shall I do, that I may have eternal life?
- v17 – And he said unto him, Why callest thou me good: there is none good but one, that is, God: but if thou wilt enter unto life, keep the commandments. . . .

Further reading: - John 14:15; Revelation 22:11-14.

Compiled by: Metusela F. Albert

The serious question on the subject of "Salvation" asked by the Jewish Rich Young Ruler, needs a good answer.

JESUS gave him the answer that we all need to learn the truth about Salvation.

The keeping of the Ten Commandments is a requirement for one who thinks of going to heaven. Since JESUS gave the answer, that settles the issue about Salvation.

Dear folks, please read Revelation 21:7 & 22:12-14, in case you are still in doubt about obedience to God's law, a requirement to have eternal life.

....

OVERCOMING AND OBEDIENCE

> ### THE OBEDIENT WILL ENTER THE NEW JERUSALEM.
>
> - Revelation 21:7.
> - He that *overcometh* shall inherit all things; and I will be his God, and he shall be my son.
>
> - Revelation 22:12 & 14.
> - V12. And behold, I come quickly; and my reward is with me, to give every man according as his work shall be.
> - V14 – Blessed at they that **do** his commandments, that they may have right to the tree of lie, and may enter in through the gates into the city.
>
> Compiled by: Metusela F. Albert

Now, the Case on Salvation is closed.

JESUS DIED <u>TO SAVE</u> THE UNGODLY.

Scripture Reading: Romans 5:6 & 8.

Many people misinterpreted Romans 5:6 and 8, to justify the unconditional love of God saved us at Calvary. They do <u>not</u> understand the difference between God's unconditional love *from* God's act of forgiveness.

Remember, JESUS already died at Calvary "to save us", <u>not</u> died and saved us unconditionally.

HOW DO WE UNDERSTAND THESE TWO VERSES IN THE BOOK OF ROMANS?

- **# 1 - Romans 5:6 says, "For when we were yet without strength, in due time <u>Christ died for the ungodly.</u>" – (KJV).**
- **NOTE: Christ died <u>to save</u> the ungodly; <u>NOT</u> died and saved the ungodly (idol worshipper).**

- **# 2 - Romans 5:8 says, "But God commendeth his love toward us, in that, while we were yet sinners, <u>Christ died for us.</u>" – (KJV).**

- **NOTE: <u>NOT</u> Christ already died for us; <u>NOT</u> Christ died and saved us.**

Compiled by: Metusela F. Albert

God loves us with an unconditional love while we are still living in sin. Amen.

Don't forget, God will <u>not</u> forgive us while we are living "in" sin. Forgiveness is a gift from God when we confess and repent of our sins.

If forgiveness will <u>*not*</u> be granted to the unrepentant sinner, then forget about the gift of Salvation because it will not happen.

There is NO such thing as God loves the ungodly and saves them while they are living in sin. It is that simple!

PROFESSED CHRISTIANS must stop promoting these Eight (8) FALSE doctrines relating to SALVATION, as listed below.

1. **When JESUS died at Calvary, he saved everyone. (FALSE).**

2. **Your past, present, and future sins, were already forgiven at Calvary by JESUS' death before you were born. (FALSE).**

3. **Salvation is by faith alone without obedience to God's law. (False).**

4. **One does not have to obey God to be saved. (FALSE).**

5. **The Ten Commandments were given only for the Jewish people. (FALSE).**

6. **God changed the Sabbath from Saturday to Sunday. (FALSE).**

7. **The New Covenant is to love our neighbor, not about keeping God's Ten Commandments. (FALSE).**

8. **Obedience is the fruit of Salvation. (FALSE).**

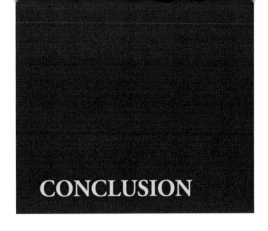

CONCLUSION

The doctrine about Salvation is misunderstood by Professed Christians because most people don't read the Scriptures in the Context. Besides that, others don't read the Scriptures because they are too busy. Many people rely on the Church to do the reading and the explanation for them. The Church becomes the truth teller. Well, the truth teller can become the agent of the devil in subtle twists.

We need to learn from one another, and when we see a certain truth presented and explained differently from our beliefs, we need to analyze it and change our beliefs, if necessary. We must keep an open mind and a humble heart to swallow our pride and accept the new explanation.

Truth is progressive, not stagnant. Truth will always remain the truth. Truth is not based on the quantity of people who believed it. The many people who believed a certain doctrine does not mean it is the truth. When Noah preached about the flood for one hundred and twenty years, only eight (8) people entered the Ark and were saved. It was not the quantity of people, but the quality of people.

I hope this Book you are reading is of help to you in some way.

For your information, the book you are holding is my 11th book. Listed below are the other TEN books I wrote that may be of interest to you and your friends. Again, Thank you.

PUBLISHED ON MARCH 04, 2011

PUBLISHED ON JUNE 01, 2021

....

THERE IS NO TRINITY GOD IN HEAVEN.

BOOK - PUBLISHED ON
DECEMBER 16, 2020

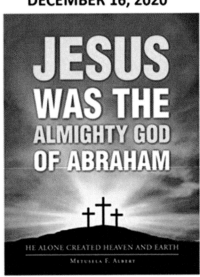

BOOK - PUBLISHED ON
JANUARY 22, 2021

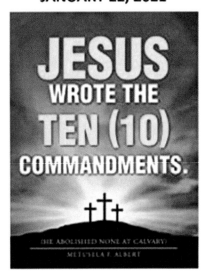

BOOK - PUBLISHED ON
SEPTEMBER 12, 2021

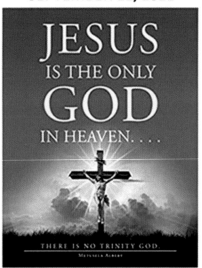

....

PUBLISHED ON AUGUST 17, 2021.

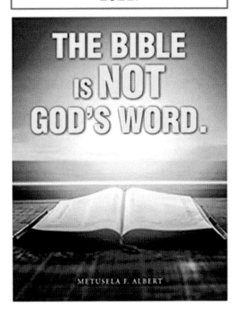

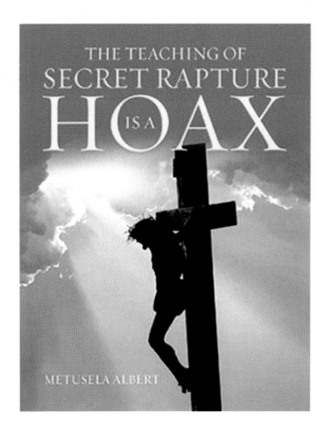

BOOK # 8

PUBLISHED ON MARCH 21, 2023.

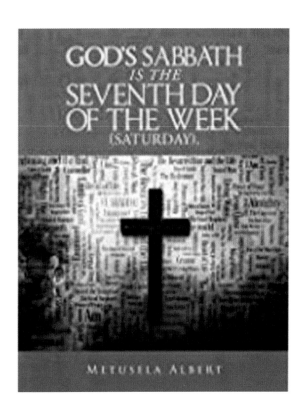

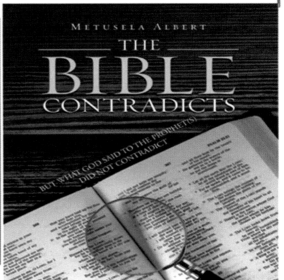

Today is Sunday, August 15, 2024.

THE MANUSCRIPT FOR MY 12ᵀᴴ BOOK IS ABOUT TO FINISH AND READY TO GO FOR PUBLISHING BY XLIBRIS PUBLISHING COMPANY.

THE TITLE OF MY 12TH BOOK IS – "GOD DID NOT HAVE A SON IN HEAVEN."

Most people still have not understood yet that John 1:1 and John 3:16 were incorrect. Stay tuned. Thanks.

I AM ABOUT TO COMPLETE WRITING MY 12ᵀᴴ BOOK.

• BOOK TITLE:
• "GOD DID NOT HAVE A SON IN HEAVEN".
(John 1:1 and 3:16 were wrong).
....
NOTE: John advocated the DUALITY and the TRINITY GOD. He contradicted what God said in Isaiah 43:10-11; 44:6, 24; 49:16.

Compiled by: Metusela F. Albert

THE END.

Printed in the United States
by Baker & Taylor Publisher Services